BEYOND BORDERS
WITH SAINT LUKE

Contents

THE CHARLES R. COIL COLLOQUIUM

ABOUT THE CHARLES R. COIL COLLOQUIUM

The Charles R. Coil Colloquium began at Heritage Christian University in the spring of 2010. The Colloquium is an annual one-day event, hosted by Friends of the Overton Memorial Library, designed to enrich the intellectual climate of Heritage Christian University, its constituency, and the greater academic community. Leaders in the various academic disciplines related to the graduate and undergraduate curricula at Heritage Christian University are invited to share their expertise.

FOREWORD

The publication of this series of lectures is significant for two reasons. It is the first Charles R. Coil Colloquium, and it is the last series of lectures that Prof. Frederick W. Danker ever gave.[1] The Charles Coil Colloquium is held each year during the spring semester in the Overton Memorial Library on the campus of Heritage Christian University (Florence, Alabama). The lectures are named in honor of the university's second president, Charles Raymond Coil (1929–1994), who served as president from 1971 until his retirement in 1989. President Coil spared no cost in order to provide those students who came to the university for training with the best education possible. And, he insisted that during their education students develop "an international view" of the church and of their role as a minister, as well as of the

---

1. Dr. Danker did continue to give a few *single* lectures here and there after his appearance at the Coil Colloquium, the last such single lecture being at the Society of Biblical Literature's annual meeting in San Francisco on November 29, 2011 in a session on the International Syriac Language Project. However, his lectures at the Coil Colloquium were the last *series* of lectures that he ever gave.

world and its history. Because he wanted to give them an "international" education, it is fitting that for the first Coil Colloquium the university invited an internationally famous biblical scholar like Dr. Danker.

Dr. Frederick William Danker (1920–2012) was known as the world's premier scholar of the Greek New Testament in the field of lexicography. His great *A Greek–English Lexicon of the New Testament and Other Early Christian Literature* (3rd ed.; Chicago/London: University of Chicago Press, 2000), based on the lexical work of Walter Bauer, is simply a "must" for every serious student of the New Testament.[2] His book *Multipurpose Tools for Bible Study*, first published in 1960, has served as a guide for countless ministers and students of the Bible.[3] *The Concise Greek–English Lexicon of the New Testament* (with Kathryn Krug; Chicago/London: University of Chicago Press, 2009) was his last publication during his lifetime. This present

---

2. So writes Gordon Fee in *New Testament Exegesis: A Handbook for Students and Pastors* (3rd ed.; Louisville/London: Westminster John Knox, 2002), p. 83, and I heartily agree with this judgment.

3. Still available in its latest form as *Multipurpose Tools for Bible Study* ([4th] rev. and expd. ed.; Minneapolis: Fortress, 1993; with CDROM, 2003).

volume of lectures will most likely be his last publication, offered posthumously now to the public eight
years after he delivered them.

This first installment in the Coil Colloquium was
held on Friday, April 9, 2010, in the Overton Memorial
Library at Heritage Christian University. Dr. Danker
spoke from 9:00 a.m. to 3:00 p.m., with a break only
for chapel and lunch. While this volume accurately
conveys Dr. Danker's words, the printed lectures can
hardly capture the great excitement that attended this
first Coil Colloquium. Many came to hear Dr. Danker
speak, some traveling hundreds of miles. Electricity
had already filled the air when Dr. Danker's deep, reso-
nating voice broke the silence and commanded everyone's attention.

Dr. Danker was eminently qualified to speak on the
Gospel of Luke, having written two commentaries on
the Third Gospel as well as several related articles.[4] His

4. Danker's two commentaries on Luke are *Jesus and the
New Age: A Commentary on the Third Gospel* (St. Louis: Clayton
Publishing House, 1972; rev. and expd. ed.; Minneapolis:
Fortress Press, 1988); and *Luke* (Proclamation Commentary;
Philadelphia: Fortress Press, 1976; rev. ed., 1987). Dr. Danker
had also written several related articles like "The Endangered
Benefactor in Luke-Acts," in *SBLSP* 20 (ed. Kent Harold
Richards; Chico, Calif.: Scholars Press, 1981), 39–48; "Imaged

thorough and unequaled knowledge of Luke's original language became obvious to everyone in attendance at the lectures, just as it will become obvious to the careful reader of this volume. New insights and a fuller understanding of Luke's Gospel await you within the pages of this book.

Dr. Danker was thrilled to be a part of this first series of the Coil Colloquium, and he felt very indebted to the Overton Memorial Library and to Heritage Christian University for making possible this last opportunity to share with others his thoughts on the Third Gospel from a wealth of knowledge accumulated over seventy years of study, a period longer than many people live. And at the age of eighty-nine, Dr. Danker was still in his prime. His mind was just as agile and sharp as ever on this occasion. His deep gratitude for this last opportunity was shown in his leaving his entire personal library, consisting of over 7,600 books (many of them rare), as well as over 6,000 journals and files of papers, to the Overton Memorial Library, with the blessing of

---

through Beneficence," in *Reimaging the Death of the Lukan Jesus* (ed. Dennis D. Sylva; BBB 73; Franfurt am Main: Anton Hain, 1990), pp. 57–67; "Luke 16:16—An Opposition Logion," *JBL* 77 (1958): 231–43; and "Theological Presuppositions of St. Luke," *CurTM* 4 (1977): 98–103.

his daughter, Kathie. All students of God's Word should be grateful to the Overton Memorial Library and to Heritage Christian University for publishing this volume of lectures.

David H. Warren, Th.D.

Montgomery, Alabama

February 2, 2018

I

After being in Florence for several days now, I am thinking to myself this is a very worldly place. You have Target and Applebee's. You have everything that we have on Grand Boulevard in the neighborhood where I live. Therefore, when I return to St. Louis and people ask what and where is Florence, now I will tell them that they are going to feel the way they felt when Tom Brokaw talked about Midwest America. We are all linked on a journey together. So, I will tell them this is a very worldly place, but it's in a way out of this world, because it is a marvelous place to live and the people I met, I will say, especially you here at Heritage Christian University, know that there is another place that is the world of God, the God who makes sure that we are able to make it through this world. And it's along these lines that I am going to be speaking about "the things fulfilled among us."

I notice that a number of you have your New Testaments, and the logical place to start is where Luke begins with the Prologue of the Gospel. In the course of this presentation, you will notice a few terms that may be unusual to you, especially when I speak about the *auditors* of Luke rather than the readers. We are readers, but in Luke's time, those who received his message were auditors because, naturally, very few people had a copy of his book or his two books, which we call Luke and Acts. The auditors were those in the congregations or gatherings of the early Christians, and they would not be accustomed to doing what we do in our various universities or seminaries—stopping at every word and wondering what in the world is this person talking about. We, as students of the word, must linger at every point in order to determine whether we have understood it correctly. One of the first rules that we have to set for ourselves is that the text is really quite understandable, because people hearing the text that we spend a great deal of labor on in order to understand it, knew the language. Another important principle to remember is that any book in the Bible and any letter or historical work, to use the word historical in a very general sense, would be readily understandable by those who were listening, because the writer of a book of this kind would have designed it for average people, unsophisticated people, in general. Instead of highly technical diction, it would be written in a way that they could understand it. Thus, these writers are not writing for us in the first place, and the higher we get in our learning process, the more distance we develop between ordinary people, who speak average language, and ourselves.

Luke lets us know right from the start that he knows how to write quite sophisticated Greek, but immediately after the fourth verse he moves into *people talk* and, in this case, the narrative way in which the Old Testament is written, taking up where the writers of the Hebrew Scriptures left off. So, we have to get accustomed to the kinds of terminology Luke employs, for example, the kind of people talk that Roman officials used. Thus, he will talk about Judeans whereas, we use the term *the Jews*. That's an anachronistic English term. Judeans are Israelites, and they are persons who are in tune with Moses and the traditions connected with Moses. Therefore, I will refer to either Judeans or Israelites in my presentation. And, for those who are not Israelites, or who are Hellenized Israelites, I will use the designation Hellenic or Hellenes.

St. Luke's book is the story about what God has brought to a climax in history. Luke makes this very clear in his very first sentence: "In as much as many have taken in hand to draw up a recital about matters fulfilled among us, exactly as they handed them over to us who from the beginning were eyewitnesses and helpers in the story." The story, the *logos*, the word—now in English, the word, "word," has many senses, and it does as well in Greek. But, when Luke says, "those who were helpers in the word," he means helpers in the story. The Bible contains God's story. And when he says, "the things fulfilled among us," he's talking about events that have taken place but that are marked by a terminating point. That is, something that God has had in mind has now come to fruition. So, it's God's story. And these matters were handed down by eyewitnesses and helpers in the story, that is, those who helped to get the story of God out. And so he says, "I resolved in as much as I had followed everything from the beginning to draw it up for you in orderly fashion," that is, in a connected account, "most excellent Theophilus so that you might have insight about the stories"—note the plural of logos is used—"of the stories and have certainty about them." The idea is that the stories have come to you in different forms, and you may be a little confused at points, because there are disagreements in how one thing fits in with another. Well, Luke says, I am here to give you an account that will help you get it all together. And, that's what we are about to do. To reflect that interest on the part of Luke in behalf of Theophilus to you at this point in your history of working on trying to understand this text.

So, St. Luke's book is the story about what God has brought to a climax in the history of the early community of followers of Jesus. In Acts 1:1–8, it is clear that God is the prime mover of what marked the fulfillment of a long process in the history of God's people. Jesus is the chief agent in the implementing of God's program. To make this joint enterprise meaningful to his publics, Luke writes in a way that will resonate with those firmly rooted in Mosaically-oriented tradition and culture and also with those more deeply absorbed in cultural patterns marked especially by the influence of Hellas. It's important to understand this, because there are so many peculiar ideas in circulation that Luke, for example, is trying to take up the Hellenic cause at the expense of Israelites.

Luke is probably a converted Mosaically-oriented Israelite, but he knows the world into which God moved with God's truth. Therefore, he's not writing to his congregation only. Luke has bigger game in mind. He is writing for publics in different places. And since his message is directed to people in many different places, he's going to be speaking the kind of language or using as a sounding block the kinds of ideas and processes of thinking that fit the way a person processes new material. So, how is he going to reach both the Mosaically-oriented elements in his publics and those who are more Hellenically-oriented? Luke's going to use models that these people, regardless of whether they are Israelites or Hellenes, will immediately recognize and therefore know what he's up to. In the case of the Hellenically-oriented, the dominant social model was the person of extraordinary performance, who renders public service in an especially meritorious fashion and is recognized with a variety of awards frequently noted in an inscription carved on a stone pillar and authorized by a political entity. I translated such inscriptions in my book titled *Benefactor*. These kinds of inscriptions would be written on stone. Why stone? Because that's forever. If you are giving an award, you want future generations to know about it. That's why you have the Charles R. Coil Colloquium. You don't want the name Charles Coil to disappear from history. When I was in Tripoli, Greece this last summer, it was a town like yours, a real modern town with many parks. I walked around the town and, everywhere I went, I saw statues and pillars with the busts of the heroes of the town, mayors and others—ordinary people, who had risen to some degree of prominence. This is a modern example of the process of thanksgiving to patrons and to persons who have rendered meritorious service.

So, in ancient times, physicians could be sure to receive honors, if they rendered laudable service to their hometowns. In the time of Eutychides, for instance, there was this decree of the people of Aigelia:

> WHEREAS Anaxippos, the son of Alexander and physician appointed by the Assembly, has conducted himself in praiseworthy fashion for many years both in his profession and in his life and spared no effort as he brought numerous citizens safely through serious diseases, including (apparently) terminal cases; therefore, in order that the People might continue to be known for expressing appropriate appreciation to those who choose to be their benefactors, and in order that physicians to come might show themselves all the more zealous in meeting the needs of the People, be it RESOLVED by the People of Aigelia, to commend Anaxippos for the warm concern he shows [in all the assistance he continually renders.][1]

There was also a person named Opramoas, who was notable for so many contributions that it was said of him that he seemed to treat his bank account as one that had all the people of the province as joint creditors.

---

1. Frederick W. Danker, *Benefactor: Epigraphic Study of a Graeco-Roman and New Testament Semantic Field* (St. Louis: Clayton, 1982), 59.

He gave so much money, put on so many contests, and repaired so many temples that his awards were recognized in a series of inscriptions that took me 40 pages to translate. And throughout, you have testimonies from the emperor of the time, Hadrian, and from many prominent leaders in the provinces in Lycia.

And, in modern times, in President Harry Truman's hometown of Independence, Missouri, there is an inscription that was written on a piece of marble that came from a temple in Athens, Greece. You can't even pick up a chip of marble from the Parthenon or you would be arrested, but they sent President Truman a whole piece of marble with the following inscription:

> The People of Greece resolves that Harry Truman, Most Illustrious President of the United States of North America, be a proxenos of the Hellenes in recognition of his arete, his distinguished leadership, and of his friendship toward Hellas and for all his endeavors in the interest of world peace.[2]

President Truman was to be a *proxenos* or a representative of the interests of another person or group of people. In ancient Greece, the proxenos was one that lived in another country, who would look out for the interests of the exporter of goods so that this exporter

2. Ibid., 236.

didn't have to go through all the red tape for which every country was famous. This would expedite and improve the exporter's bottom line. The inscription is given in recognition of Truman's *arete*, that's a Greek word that describes a person of extraordinary merit, or one who expresses his patriotism in special service to a particular province, city, or group. And so, the people of Greece resolved that Truman be recognized for all of his endeavors and especially in the interest of world peace, and:

> "(It is further resolved) that a copy of this decree be inscribed on a stone taken from the sanctuary of Athena Victory on the Akropolis at Athens, with said stone to be presented to President Truman, proxenos of the Hellenes, in Washington on the day when the great Liberation Anniversary is observed in Greece; and that envoys be chosen from our frontline forces in the (current) war, who shall deliver this decree to the President, together with a little gift, to remind him always of the friendship and gratitude of the Hellenes.[3]

When I was working on my big dictionary, this is the kind of language I encountered all over the place, especially in Paul's letters. That's why it's necessary to study the people's language. Again, this is all written in very

3. Ibid.

simple Greek, because people who can't read will ask somebody else who happens to have had a little education to read it. And, so it was in my case on one occasion that a particular inscription was surrounded by some information in Greek, but it was written in the kind of handwriting that I didn't recognize fully, especially the names. I, who was presumed to know Greek, had to ask a farmer who was visiting and taking in the sites, and he read it with ease. So, keep that in mind when you are reading St. Paul's letters. Think in terms of somebody who does not have a college education, standing over your shoulder and saying, "Well, that's very simple. It just means this." A little humility is required, which is what Paul himself constantly advises to his auditors.

These honorees do not fall under a single categorical term. That is, the word benefactor is only one term. A benefactor is a person of good will or one who has rendered some sort of meritorious service. The recipients themselves are principally described with action verbs and with reference to specific obligations undertaken in behalf of their city. Notice, when St. Paul writes about Syntyche, for instance, he mentions she had rendered valuable service to his mission. Abundant are adverbs specifying quality performance.

Political considerations also lead to the exchange of inscribed messages between states with expressions of gratitude for courtesies extended and with assurance of reciprocity. In general, the process of expressing honor and appreciation for service that is rendered may be classified as *Public Recognition of Special Merit*, though for convenience, the recipients may be termed benefactors. For Luke, God the Father of Jesus Christ is the supreme benefactor, and Jesus is the great benefactor, because Jesus is always carrying out what his heavenly Father intends for him to do. But, it's God's story. We have to keep that in mind, because we followers of Jesus Christ tend to get in so many debates and arguments about who God is. So, Luke tells us who God is and that whatever talk we engage in is first of all to be about the God and Father of our Lord Jesus Christ.

The theme of beneficence in Greek literature carries over to numerous lesser entities. For example, regarding heads of state, you have emperors called *god*. Now, in support of his literary strategy of focusing on God as protagonist and all the action that follows in his account, Luke ensures that his Mosaic, as well as the more Hellenically-oriented auditors find mutuality under a canopy of exposure to a common Mediterranean world experience. And that's the way he gets them together.

Hence, in the first three chapters, Luke includes a number of motifs that reflect the interests of the earliest recorders "of things fulfilled among us." Such themes include angelic visits, signs, and portents. All these make an impression on people, when they hear history books read to them. This is the case, whether it's Tacitus of Rome or Thucydides of Athens. All these would create an atmosphere of involvement in events transcending normal experience.

The better historians in both Roman and Hellenic centers would be very cautious about what we call or tend to call supernatural events, which, I think, is an erroneous expression. I prefer the word transcendent, that is, they transcend normal experience. But, when you are dealing with one who already transcends normal experience, namely the God and Father of our Lord Jesus Christ, and you are writing the way events are recorded in an older book or set of books like what we call the Old Testament, in order to communicate the identity of God and the identity of Jesus the Christ, then you must incorporate angelic visits, signs, and portents. These provide a linguistic event experience for the auditors, because the only way they can understand is through what they already know. The only way we understand anything is in terms of what we already know,

BEYOND BORDERS WITH SAINT LUKE

and when something new comes up, then we have to go through all the study of grammar and what we call exegeses, involving us in a hermeneutical task. So, instead of intruding personally with an intellectual analysis, Luke adopts the hermeneutical device of using agents within his account to interpret the larger story, which he calls the *logos*. There are seven of these messages, observations, or conclusions in the first three chapters. So, we must get in the habit of letting Luke tell us what Luke is saying, because he provides a hermeneutical way for us to get into the details, and if we are stuck on some of the particulars, well, you just read on, and he'll explain it.

The first message is delivered by a heavenly messenger to Zachariah (Luke 1:5–25). The subject is the significance of his son John. John's importance is expressed in a number of ways. Many will experience joy because of his birth. A similar thought was expressed on an inscription in honor of Caesar Augustus in 9 BC. In this inscription, Augustus is praised, as if, for ordinary people, it is as though creation had just begun, and people thought to themselves that if it were not for his birth, they might as well not be living. He brought joy to people. So, John the Baptizer will be great before the Lord. The term "great" would make Luke's auditors think of Alexander the Great. That is, John's going to be a person about whom the kinds of things said in these inscriptions should be expressed. This means that he will be recognized by God for an especially distinguished service as messenger. In other words, he is a person of exceptional merit and will be a benefactor of many. Importantly, he will be filled with the Holy Spirit. What does that mean? That means primarily that he's a person especially dedicated to God. And, to show that he's in a special category, he will drink no wine or beer. References to the Holy Spirit are a strong feature throughout Luke-Acts. Luke's two volumes contain more references to the Holy Spirit than do the books of Matthew, Mark, and John all together. John will direct many Israelites to the Lord their God in the spirit and functioning power of Elijah. I emphasize functioning power, because the word *dunamis* is usually rendered "power" as such and that suggests power plays and the like in our language. But, in Greek, the term means ability to function and, especially if it involves people, to function in a way that is beneficial to others.

Now, portents are also an important feature of the narrative. They are prevalent in recitals of great men in antiquity. John's approaching birth is announced by a heavenly messenger. That in itself is a portent. A portent accompanies Zachariah's entry on the scene too. He will be mute, because he did not take the angel's message at face value. This is an ominous note. In Luke's subsequent narrative, there will be a good deal of unbelief exposed, but God proceeds with his timetable anyway.

Message two is the message of the angel Gabriel to Mary (Luke 1:26–38). That in itself is another portent. He states that Mary has experienced a special favor or benefit from God. She will bear a child and call his name Jesus. Luke's auditors, Gentiles as well as Israelites, would recognize the relative superiority of Jesus through the use of the Greek word *megas* ("great"). Associating Jesus with Joshua, the deliverer for the Israelites, is significant for the Mosaically-oriented, and Jesus will also be recognized by the Hellenes as having relative superiority. Jesus will be John's superior. So, as a latter-day Joshua, Jesus now, through the message of Gabriel, enjoys the exceptional status as "Son of the Most High," whereas, Zachariah talks about his son as "the prophet of the Most High" (Luke 1:76 NRSV). God awards Jesus the throne of his ancestor David. Mary asks, "How will this take place?" She has had no intimate relations with a man (v. 34). Her question is different from that of Zachariah, who asked for a sign. Mary simply asks how, which all women would immediately recognize and would naturally ask. Zachariah's was a case of demanding a sign and making God declare to an ordinary mortal the grounds on which something should be done. To Luke's auditors, the extraordinary indication of Jesus' special distinction is the circumstance under which he was conceived. The second part of the message concerns Elizabeth. It is accompanied by the portent of a woman, who is beyond child bearing age, and who is about to bear a son.

Message three is delivered by Mary herself (Luke 1:46–55). Her words are a recitation of divine beneficence. She shows her faith in God's fulfillment of his ancient promise to Abraham, who receives much notice in Luke's account. Her message is a preview of Zachariah's interpretation of the significance of the events that are about to take place. Israel's big moment has arrived. Luke's auditors know that things have not turned out exactly the way that Israelites would have liked regarding the arrival of the Messianic Age, and it will be a stumbling block for them. So, you have this glowing account of what's going to happen in favor of Israel, but it doesn't seem to happen. Well, you have to read Luke's story all the way through to the end. Abraham's offspring, however, will emerge with a display of God's mercy.

Mary's statement about the high and the low-ly focuses attention on the theme of resocialization. Resocialization is the only way that I can describe this whole approach in Luke's Gospel in which he talks about, as Mary does, the theme of love, directives to take care of the poor, and to bring those on the outside to the inside. Regarding these things, God is savior. So, Luke has numerous narratives in which notation is made about being saved, a word which is so often loosely bandied about. Are you saved? Well, in what way? In Luke, it has to do very often with being saved from illness or other conditions. Luke's story of Jesus' activity is the answer to the question—how does God show salvation and mercy?

Message four is delivered by Zachariah (Luke 1:68–80) with focus on the celebration of divine beneficence in terms of deliverance from oppression. This is central to the observation that God fulfills his promises to his ancient people, and Zachariah's son, John, is to prepare God's path before him. Included in God's beneficence is forgiveness of sins and light to those who sit in darkness and in the shadow of death. Examples of these benefits will be noted by Luke in his subsequent accounts.

Message five is delivered by an angel and then by a chorus of angels (Luke 2:8–20). The birth of the great king in the royal family of David, as did the birth of Caesar Augustus, spells great joy. It is for all the people. The reference to all as beneficiaries is a common motif in ancient inscriptions. "So and so did this for everybody regardless of their station in life." It relates to exceptional persons of merit. Whenever you run into this idea—that so and so did this for all—recognize immediately that at this point Hellenic ears would perk up. And, "Jesus is born a savior in the city of David" would immediately get the attention of Israelites. Notice the kingdom is always at hand. As in Acts 2:36, the identity of Jesus as Joshua and then as Christ are the two titles favored by Luke for Jesus. Jesus as Lord is accountable only to God. A supporting cast of heavenly messengers proclaims the appropriate response to the extraordinary divine benefit. Glory is the proper response to the supreme deity.

This is a call to all beneficiaries to recognize God as one to be honored, who wins renown for his priceless benefits. That's what the idea of glory is all about. It's about a person or a group that receives appropriate recognition for being extraordinary in merit and worthy of praise. So, all in Israel should be primarily interested in removing any hindrance to full acceptance by God. And, Luke is not a writer who tells congregations that

God is out to get them. God is a benefactor, who is out to bring Israel to a position, whereby Israel will recognize itself as recipient of glory. Why do Olympic athletes expend so much effort? It's to receive glory and to be recognized for their exceptional merit as athletes. So, heaven is not a remote area disconnected from everyday human experience.

A sixth message is expressed by Simeon in Luke 2:25–35. He acknowledges the theme of fulfillment announced in the preamble. He celebrates God's rescuing action, as exhibited in the baby he enfolds in his arms. And, it echoes the recognition of the kind of broad outreach associated with benefactors. Notice this word "all" that I spoke about. Jesus is not only for one particular people, but for all peoples. This insight anticipates recital of Luke's theme of broad outreach of the gospel. Israel's participation in that outreach will redound to its glory.

The seventh message (Luke 2:38) is only cited indirectly by Luke. It's assigned to Anna (Gk. Hannah), an aged prophet. She spoke to all who were awaiting the deliverance of Jerusalem. And she said, along with Simeon, as well as Zachariah and Elizabeth, that the kingdom of God is to arrive in that deliverance.

It's appropriate at this point to comment on Luke's emphasis on the Holy Spirit. Luke uses the term *spirit* in several ways. Primarily the word refers to the non-physically expressive aspect of an entity. That is, one cannot see the entity, but one knows of its existence through the way the entity functions. Thus, God is known through his effective activity. Frequently, the personal character of such activity is expressed by the word *holy*, an especially significant quality that produces an extraordinary effect, like the virgin conception of Jesus. Notice, I did not say virgin birth, because Luke talks about the conception that is brought about through a special action of God. The Holy Spirit will come upon Mary. The explanatory phrase that follows states that this is no ordinary spirit, but the very spirit of the highest one there is, namely God, who will function in the manner of a shadow to bring about Mary's pregnancy. The maneuver is so special that Jesus will be identified as the "Son of God." Other instances of the functioning evidence of God, that is God's dunamis, appear with frequency in the infancy narratives, all the way through the end of Luke 2.

The presentation of these messages concludes with a story about the child Jesus at the age of twelve. His precociousness amazes pedagogues in the Temple. Ancient rhetoricians recommended to writers dealing with the lives of extraordinary persons that they include stories illustrating their youthful precocity. By including this episode about the intelligence of Jesus, Luke helps his Hellenic auditors recognize that Jesus is indeed an exceptional person worthy of highest adulation. Like Jesus, Opramoas, the aforementioned millionaire from Lycia, was recognized as one who from a young age showed enormous promise as a person of merit.[4] At the same time, the dialogue with Jesus' mother draws attention to a relationship that transcends earthly relationships, namely, the one with his heavenly Father.

The literary transition to Jesus' main occupation of implementing God's great plan of salvation for Israel and for the world has now been made. And, the next scene shows us the entry of the son of Zachariah as advance man for Jesus. For, God is the supreme politician, and Jesus is the great politician. That is, they are in charge of all his dunamis and all the functioning power and ability to bring about that which is in the best interest of the greatest number of people—that is to the

4. "And (whereas) Opramoas himself, adorned from his earliest youth with arete and good judgment, has already distinguished himself for illustrious service in his home town" (Danker, *Benefactor*, p. 113).

world. As I mentioned, John the Baptizer is the advance man, and this is our assurance that the way for the rescue of humanity is about to be undertaken. Auditors of both Mosaic and more Hellenically-oriented backgrounds and traditions would be impressed by one's association with political figures. Thus, God is the supreme politician. But now, we see a number of political figures, who appear in the story of the arrival of John the Baptizer. And by doing it in this way, Luke presents John's appearance as a world-shaking event.

The citation of Isaiah 40:3–5 would contribute to this impressiveness. The people of the Mediterranean Basin respected confirmation from antiquity. That's why they tended to confer special favor on Israelites. Alterations of terrain as noted in this citation from Isaiah are typical in descriptions of the arrival of a head of state. The valleys will be leveled to make it easier for the emperor's officials to get to the destination. The universal aspect of God's saving activity (all will see God's saving activity) is thematic in Luke. John, here, has met his obligation of introducing Jesus, who is now the main figure in God's outreaching program. He graciously withdraws himself, does John, and puts the spotlight on Jesus. Then, Luke removes John completely from the current scene with the notation that Herod Antipas imprisoned him, although Luke does not include the gory details that Mark does.

Greek rhetoricians advised writers to include impressive genealogies in descriptions of great men. This is very important to know as you try to decipher why and how the genealogy in Luke is different from that of Matthew. You must pursue Luke's line of presentation of the material, his "orderly account," by recognizing that the material is presented in such a way that Israelites and Hellenically-oriented publics would readily know what was going on. And since rhetoricians indicated that impressive genealogies are important, Luke obliges. In fact, he traces Jesus' connections back through Adam, with God himself as the climactic entity. In similar fashion, heads of state were connected from time immemorial to deities. Thus, Luke concludes his introductory presentation of Jesus as the Great Benefactor, who transcends all benefactors except God himself. The rest of Luke's Gospel and the book of Acts will show how Jesus' role plays out.

After carefully delineating the personhood of Jesus, Luke outlines in broad strokes the nature of the task that lies before him. Here, we come to the temptation of one who wants to be remembered as the Great Politician. The Great One, whose purpose is to bring all humanity under the roof of God's all-encompassing outreach, encounters one who considers himself second in command to God. Luke identifies him as the *diabolos*—the Divider. His three temptations prepare Luke's auditors for themes that are explored in the main body of the Evangelist's story. Notice how all these introductory accounts prepare us for what Luke has to say in the rest of his Gospel and in the book of Acts. There is first of all the importance of the spiritual over the material. Then, there is the matter of political power and the test of God's concern and care for one who is in harm's way. After Jesus' rejection of Diabolos' attempts to steer him off his path of commitment to his heavenly Father, Diabolos holds off and looks forward to another opportune time. This comment acts as an introductory note to the time when Jesus goes through the process of judgment managed by a variety of power elements, as they unleash attacks on Jesus later in Luke's Gospel. For instance, it is stated in Luke 22:3 that Satan entered into Judas, called Iscariot, who was one of Jesus' cabinet members, the Twelve. So, in this series of infancy narratives and then the temptations, we have all of the script that follows in Luke-Acts. All the players that we encounter there have already been anticipated.

After the temptation scene in Luke 4:1–13, Jesus goes to Nazareth and makes his inaugural address. God is directing him to carry out his heavenly Father's program for outreach and rescue of the marginalized, release to captives, and sight to the blind, and to send off the oppressed with relief. We're talking salvation here—a proclamation of God's welcoming time. Jesus then rolls up the scroll of Isaiah and declares, "It all begins today." He uses the word *sēmeron* ("today"), which had previously been spoken by the angel of the Lord to the shepherds (Luke 2:11). The people of Nazareth were impressed by Jesus' declaration. They were delighted at the premise of God's special favor. Jesus is from their own town. But, how are they to know what he can do and what his inaugural speech calls for? He said it all begins today. Well then, they want to see a few samples of the kind of wonders Jesus performed in Capernaum. But, Luke hasn't told the story at Capernaum yet. The story involving Capernaum takes place earlier in time but later in Luke's text. Jesus declines their request, for they are demanding a sign. They want a portent, rather than a beneficent act of God. Therefore, he makes reference to the experiences of Elijah and Elisha in ancient Israel. God selects the recipients of his mercy. Jesus does not act on his own just to be glorified as a wonderworker.

The true prophet acts on discretion from God. Not all widows received special treatment through Elijah—only the widow of Zarephath. And only Naaman was cured of leprosy through Elisha. Jesus said to his townspeople, "I tell you no prophet is welcome in his own homeland." With that saying, he charted his future in Israel. He would face constant obstruction and critique from the elite leaders in Israel's religious circles for carrying out the program announced in Nazareth.

Luke's very next narrative then brings Capernaum to the fore. Notice, Luke is writing *kathexēs* or an "orderly account." This does not demand chronological sequence necessarily, but Luke arranges his material in an orderly fashion. He follows his own hermeneutical technique of forecasting what's coming down the pike. What happened at Capernaum was the healing of one who was tormented by a demon. Diabolos had claimed to have jurisdiction over all the kingdoms. He's the Satan, also. And those of you who have read Job carefully will note that Satan is an ally of God, who helps God do his chores on earth. But, Jesus invades Diabolos' own territory with authority given him by his heavenly Father. So, he ranked far above Satan. Jesus is the Son of God without impediment.

At this point, Luke relates the story of Simon in his fishing boat. Crowds were mobbing Jesus. He sees two fishing boats. The fishers had gone out of them and were washing their nets. Jesus climbed into one of the boats, which happened to belong to Simon. Jesus asked Simon to move a bit offshore, and then he began to instruct the crowds. When Jesus finished teaching, Simon, after some protest, humored Jesus' request for a launch out into deep waters. *Voilà!* So many fish! Their nets were beginning to tear. The fishers called for help and quite soon both boats were so loaded with fish that they began to take on water. Jesus is not stingy. He's a true benefactor. He loads people down with benefits. Simon, also now referred to as Peter, is not used to dealing with such a generous God, and he is now into religion, and says, "Depart from me. I am not worthy to be in your company. I'm one they call a sinner." Jesus resocializes him on the spot: "No need to fear, you are going to have a new status. From now on, you will be catching people alive." He was introducing Peter to God's outreaching mission and giving him a new identity. He was no longer a sinner. It was a malleable right of conviction and absolution. In Israelite society, the term "sinner" applied to those who didn't really know too much about keeping the Law. At Nazareth, Jesus spoke about the exceptional leper who was healed in the time of Elisha. Now, in one of Israel's towns, a leper was healed upon his request to Jesus. Jesus ordered him to show himself to the priest by way of testimony to them. That is, they would have the opportunity to draw the conclusion that God was at work in a special way.

We now come to the story in Luke 6, where the disciples are cracking grain kernels on the Sabbath to satisfy their hunger. Jesus states that David and his band even ate the showbread, which only the priests had authority to eat. Notice, Jesus is free to interpret the Law, which the Pharisees invoke in order to maintain their position of power over the ordinary people and their isolation from the average Israelite. The human one, the Son of Man, is God's agent and has authority over rules governing the Sabbath. And then, there is the counter development that this fragile human being, and we see his fragility at the crucifixion where his identity is being questioned, is going to be glorified. Thus, his role as great benefactor of the human cause is brought to climatic expression. That would be the moment of his *doxa*, when he is recognized as the ultimate person of merit next to the heavenly Father.

Jesus' concern for Israel continues to mount as Luke continues to tell his story. A centurion recognized Jesus'

extraordinary role. In Luke 7, he is distinguished beyond ordinary mortals in word and in deed. Word and
deed are two items that are characteristically noted
about people of exceptional merit—those who are in
high positions. Many politicians are very good at words,
but don't back the words up with deeds. And so, that is a
big item in reading these inscriptions—whether so and
so is a talker. Well, being a good speaker is highly val-
ued, but do you back it up with deeds? The centurion
sees that this is the case with Jesus as the exceptional
person. Jesus then recognized that the centurion has
displayed more faith than Israelites collectively show.

After Jesus raises a young man from the dead at Nain
in Luke 7:11–17, John the Baptizer sends a message
asking whether Jesus was the one who was to come.
Jesus gives his answer with the words from the prophet Isaiah. To have faith means to recognize that God's
program for the disadvantaged in Israel, for the sick, for
those who suffer loss through the death of a loved one,
the blind, the deaf, and the lame, is for all to receive care
through Jesus. God's agent for carrying out the covenant promises of God to Israel is Jesus. John is the one
who prepares the way for the Messiah. The Pharisees
and lawyers refuse to celebrate God's own program
outlined in the Scriptures. And so, the focus in Luke's

narrative is on the importance of recognizing the God of Israel, who is interested in carrying out the promise made to Abraham—that in him and in his offspring all nations of the earth would be blessed.

These words introduce us to the story about Simon, a Pharisee, who cannot understand how Jesus, if he is as alleged, a prophet, fails to know that the woman, who drenched Jesus' feet with perfume, dried them with her hair, and kissed them, is a notorious sinner. This is the same word that Peter used of himself, "I am a sinner," without necessarily indicating that Peter had done a lot of things wrong. This woman is notorious, however. She had learned to know who God really was through Jesus' outreach to sinners—those who were on the fringes of society from a Levitical perspective. Luke suggests that without Jesus and his mission to define God as deity by his outreach to humanity, God would have no identity. How would we even know who God is, unless we had one who could call God "Father"? And who is God, when we don't have someone like Luke or St. Paul to tell us? God would be an unknown. But, Luke also emphasizes that God is not an entity to be feared when disaster strikes.

II

In the preceding section, we looked at Luke's story from its beginning in Jerusalem to the moment when Jesus moved determinedly toward Jerusalem. Now, we begin this lecture with an examination of Luke's narrative known as the travel section or trip to Jerusalem. Then, we'll consider the narrative of the crucifixion and resurrection, followed by the story of the outreach to Israel and the nations. Scholars long ago noted the break at Luke 9:51: "When the days drew near for him to be taken up, he set his face to go to Jerusalem" (NRSV). Those of you who have your Nestle-Aland Greek New Testament or the American Bible Society Edition will see the delineation in the typeface with the section terminating at either 19:10 or 19:27. Whether it can properly be called a document, as in the title *Travel Document* that is frequently given to it, is an inquiry which lies outside the framework of this presentation.

According to Acts, the followers of Jesus were called people of "the Way." This idea is consistent with the Isaianic connection made by John the Baptizer in Luke 3:4—"prepare the way of the Lord." So, at Luke 9:51 we note the structural break, "He set his face to head toward Jerusalem." While this journeying section has been termed the Travel Document, it might more appropriately be called Luke's *Literary Journey Capsule.* The Evangelist focuses on Jerusalem as the culminating point for God's execution of his purpose that was pronounced in the Prologue of the Gospel—of the matters "fulfilled among us," namely, bringing Jesus to birth to carry out God's covenant promise to Israel and to the world.

The literary record of the journey consists of sayings and counsel punctuated by an overriding theme—Jesus does battle against demonic powers. Hence, in this travel section, Luke injects sayings of Jesus that point to Jesus' ultimate destiny in Jerusalem. As a prelude to this thematic note in the travel piece, Luke recites the Scripture as given by Jesus after Peter's affirmation that he was the Messiah. Jesus says, "the human one," also known as the Son of Man, must suffer much. This is where the matter of his fragility comes in. The human one must suffer much and be disqualified by the elders, chief priests, and scribes and be put to death and on the third day be raised. As I already pointed out, "the human one" is a better rendering than "the Son of the Man." The related plural form, "sons of men," is often used in the Old Testament in reference to human beings as mere earthlings. Also, however, it is used in the singular as one subject to fragility (Isa 51:12) and in the Septuagint, as one likened to a worm (Job 25:6). "Sons of men" is also used in Mark 3:28 and in Eph 3:5. In the New Testament, except for the use of the term by Stephen in Acts 7:56, the singular form is found only on the lips of Jesus. In the context immediately preceding the notice about Jesus' determination to make his way toward Jerusalem, Luke reported on the failure of the disciples to grasp the significance of Jesus' word about the human one being handed over to humans—notice the play on words.

John the Evangelist was principal exemplar of this kind of lack of comprehension, when he expressed pride in having discouraged a man from practicing exorcism, since the man in question did not belong to the band of the disciples. "He's not one of us," John argued. Jesus replied, "Stop preventing him. One who is not against you, disciples of mine, is on your side." It is clear that Jesus has his sights on the demolition of Satan's objectives. Regarding Jesus' attitude, you can compare Cicero's approach to Julius Caesar on behalf of his client Ligarius: "For we have often heard you assert that, while we held all men to be our opponents save those on our side, you counted all men your adherents who were not against you" (*Lig.* 11).

Jesus' first order of business is to send envoys ahead of him on the way to Jerusalem. They stop at a Samaritan village. The residents do not lay out the welcome mat, because Jesus had his mind set on Jerusalem. The two disciples ask Jesus for permission to reign down fire and consume the inhabitants. They think the same way that is characterized in many of the Old Testament stories in which those who are opposed to the Israelites are given a special show by Yahweh. They think of God as one who desires vengeance, but this is not the kind of deity that Luke is out to program. The story, including Jesus' rebuke of them, is significant for several reasons. By relating the fact that Jesus' rebuked the disciples, Luke maintains continuity with the motif that God is omniscient—he sees beyond the notion of traditional borders. God, the supreme benefactor, is there for all. Second, Luke reinforces the point that the new age that has dawned with the birth of Jesus is marked by assurance of God's mercy, not judgment. The matter of final judgment, however, will be taken up later in Luke's narrative. Third, the mission is in harmony with the concept of peace sounded by Zachariah in Luke 1:79.

Fourth, the story anticipates the outreach to Samaria in Acts 1:8 and 8:25.

The incident in Samaria marks the beginning of Jesus' trip to Jerusalem and is immediately followed by a warning about the hazards of association with Jesus. To some, association with Jesus was a mark of honor, for he was a celebrity in the eyes of many—in today's terminology, a rock star. An enthusiastic groupie says, "I will follow you wherever you go." But, Jesus begins to tell him the facts about association with him. "Foxes have dens and birds have nests, but the human one has no place to lay his head." What does that mean? In light of Luke's focus on the hazards that Jesus faces, Luke was probably thinking about the advantage that a fox has to retreat to its den when harassed, and how a bird has the safety of its nest in the trees. Jesus then initiates a conversation in outreach to another person. "Follow me," he said. "First let me bury my father" was the response. This would have been considered a normal request and a filial obligation. But Jesus tells him, "Let the dead bury their dead." The saying is a powerful declaration that the person has been offered an opportunity of a lifetime. An earth-shaking event is about to take place in Jerusalem. Others can take care of the family obligations for now, but you, directs Jesus, declare the reign of God. The third person says, "I will follow you Lord, but first let me say farewell to my family." Jesus knows the outcome. The family will try to talk him out of it. In a different context, he will speak about the risks of family pressure (Luke 14:26). So, if you wait long enough in reading Luke, you find clarification of some of these statements that seem to be incredible or very difficult. Luke is always ready with his hermeneutical tips.

Jesus, knowing the outcome, wants this would-be follower to know that company with him is dangerous business. A follower is faced with tough choices. "No one who puts his hand to the plow and looks back is suited for kingdom activity" (Luke 9:62). Plowing the straight row requires a fixed posture that keeps the end of the furrow in sight. After Jesus had sent messengers as advance men in Luke 9:52, he appointed an additional seventy for broader outreach to all the cities and sites to which he planned to go. They are to go out two by two. There are a number of ancient inscriptions indicating that the custom was to send out envoys, quite frequently two by two. Jesus is a commander-in-chief. By adopting the language of diplomatic practice, Luke maintains the pattern established at the beginning of his story. Jesus has imperial stature, and he now sends out emissaries two by two. In Acts 13:32, Barnabas and Saul will form a commissioned pair to carry out the work the Holy Spirit has assigned them to. God is the imperial personage. The envoys are told in Luke's account that they can feel free to accept provisions at whatever house they are peacefully received. The theme of reciprocity is underscored here. The envoys of the Lord bring a valuable commodity, namely salvation, and providing food and lodging is an appropriate response on the part of the recipients. They are in fact beneficiaries of their benefactor's bounty. But, the envoys are to remember their dignity too. They are to use the lodgings as headquarters for their outreach with the message of the kingdom. They are not to move around from house to house and thereby create the impression that they are itinerant beggars. They are envoys of the king. Presumably they may serve, like Elijah and Elisha, as role models. They are to heal the sick but are to guard against receiving accolades for the healings that take place. Rather, they are to tell the people: "The reign of God has come to you." Thus, Luke emphasizes God as the supreme benefactor.

The gesture of shaking off the dust from their feet is a statement made in the public square, and again, it is to be attended with the statement and proclamation: "The reign of God has come to you." Only in this case, the gesture is a solemn affirmation that they have dismissed these people, who by then had begun to be hostile. They dismissed a spectacular gift of God and must think about the consequences. You don't treat imperial envoys that way. Luke then pens a saying that he has found in his cache of sources: "I tell you, on that day it will be more tolerable for Sodom than for that town" (Luke 10:12 NRSV). The lines of the narrative are clearly in keeping with Luke's two-stage view of the reign of God. The kingdom of God, first of all, shows itself in the ministry of Jesus as a peaceful outreach to humanity—that's the theme that was announced at the beginning of the Gospel. But, too, there is a time of judgment coming, when rejection of God's offer is reviewed.

On the return of the envoys, they are proud of their successes. "Master, even the demons obey us, when we announce your name." Jesus celebrates with a smile. "It was a great sight," he says. "Satan dropping down from heaven like lightening." Translation, "Diabolos has been evicted." Then, Jesus gives them a reality check. Satan is determined. The job is not yet done. "Don't rejoice too much over your success in casting out demons, but rather rejoice that God has entered your names in the Book of Life." This was another way of saying that God has put Jesus here for that purpose—to overcome Satan.

Luke shows that this is the point by the sayings that follow in Luke 10:21–23. The Holy Spirit fills Jesus with joy, ecstatic joy, and he gives thanks to his heavenly Father for revealing God's salvation activity to those who are novices. Here, Luke gives his auditors a flashback to the angels' message to the shepherds about God's goodwill. Jesus then concludes: "You are seeing and hearing what many prophets and kings would have liked to see and hear in their own lifetimes."

In Luke 10:25–29, Jesus next points out that he is not a teacher of moral rules. An expert in the Law asks Jesus what he can do to inherit eternal life. That he, a lawyer, should ask such a question seems odd to Jesus. "What does the law tell you?" asks Jesus. The lawyer's answer is in effect a correct summary of the Mosaic code. It's all about dedicated love, ending with loving your neighbor as yourself. Well, the man has spoken well. "This do, and you shall live," Jesus concludes. But, the lawyer spoils it for himself. He's done a good lawyering job so far, except for his asking what he can do to inherit eternal life. Unfortunately, he makes a power play now, and he tries to get the matter into his own courtroom: "Just who is my neighbor?" Thus, the lawyer moves back into the legal arena that caused him to seek to embarrass Jesus in the first place. And thus, he also becomes representative of the leaders in Israel, who use their legal and cultural traditions to marginalize people. Upon listening to Jesus' story about a Samaritan, who did what a priest and Levite avoided to do for a man who was hijacked, Jesus asks the lawyer, "Who of these three was neighbor to the victim?" Thereby, he altered the lawyer's question from a standard legal question to a question about social responsibility. The lawyer replied, "The one who showed mercy to him." Loving God with all that one is shows that one knows the true character of God. The lawyer is now open to the motivating power of God. Jesus said to him "Go"—the key word in the travel section. Then, he adds, "You are to do likewise."

Upon a request by his disciples for instruction on prayer, Jesus provided them with a guideline known as The Lord's Prayer. Unfortunately, through the centuries, the guide has turned into a ritual set piece. We gather together, and when we don't know what else to say, we say The Lord's Prayer. So, paying attention to Luke's placement of this instruction within his total literary context will help uncover some of its profound significance. The prayer is not merely designed for rote recitation. The plural pronoun "us" focuses attention on the need for thoughtful awareness by Christ's followers. In effect, this prayer is a summary of the principal themes in Luke's Gospel. And if we have forgotten what those themes are, Jesus' directions about how to pray is a useful way to bring them all together.

Remember, at the age of twelve, Jesus professed his allegiance to God as his Father. The accounts between that narrative and the present recording of Jesus' prayer recommendation had included, among other topics, narratives about demons being cast out. But, Diabolos or Satan, is still very active. Jesus' followers must therefore be very wary in the face of his temptations. Security is to be found only in faithful commitment to the heavenly Father: "Father, hallowed be your name" (Luke 11:2 NRSV). Those who pray to the Father affirm that they are interested in devoting their lives to performance that enhances God's reputation. And that's what the whole idea of glorifying God is—to enhance God's renown or stature as the supreme benefactor. Father is an intimate term implying a close relationship with God. Luke's Hellenic auditors would be struck by this. For, Plato in the *Timaeus* observes: "Now to discover the Maker and Father of this Universe were a task indeed; and having discovered Him, to declare Him unto all men were a thing impossible" (*Tim.* 28).

In his temptation of Jesus, Diabolos had tried to sidetrack Jesus from devotion to God's interests by offering him worldly control—all the kingdoms of the world. Jesus tells his disciples that they are to seek to advance God's royal interests—"Your kingdom come" (Luke 11:2 NRSV). That's what the reign of God or the kingdom of God is about. Jesus tells his disciples, therefore, that they are to seek the royal interests of God, rather than their own interests. The pertinence of this line becomes apparent in light of the inclination of some of the disciples to make moves for power. Luke 9:46–48 records a dispute about who might be the greater. At Luke 10:20, Jesus chided his disciples about basking in triumph over demonic opponents. In Luke 22, he will rebuke the apostles for indulging in a competition for who's the best benefactor.

Frequent accounts in Luke's story of Jesus' obedience to his Father deal with the proper use of possessions, warning us about confidence in their support of power, and recognition of the heavenly Father's care and concern in trying circumstances. The heavenly Father, he says, takes care of birds, and he knows the needs of Jesus' followers too. Therefore, the community members assure the heavenly Father in this petition that they do look to him for their daily nourishment: "Give us each day our daily bread" (Luke 11:3 NRSV). Daily—they look to God to supply what is only needed for each day. Implied is the thought that they first focus on the reign of God and the kingdom of God. Instructions about selling all one's possessions and giving the proceeds to the poor also lie behind the inclusion of this petition. Thus, the Lord's Prayer in Luke is also a hermeneutical device for helping us to understand what else goes on subsequently in this Gospel.

God's specialty is forgiveness: "Forgive us our sins, trespasses, or the erroneous directions that we take." Thus spoke Zechariah in Luke 1:77 in reference to the essence of salvation. And forgiveness is connected to a baptism that involves repentance. Jesus declares forgiveness to a cripple and to a woman who had a bad reputation. The reciprocal idea of forgiveness is expressed by the participle of the commercial term owe, as in owing money. It's used metaphorically of being under an interpersonal obligation to "forgive everyone indebted to us" (Luke 11:4 NRSV).

The final petition, "Do not lead us to a test," is primarily an expression of humility formed as a plea that the petitioner be spared a test of their loyalty to the heavenly Father. They are to live in awareness that grievous peril awaits them at all times.

In his concluding instruction about prayer, based on the story of the pleading neighbor who knocks on his friend's door at midnight in Luke 11:5–15, Jesus speaks about being persistent in prayer. The focus is of course on the themes of the Lord's Prayer. And I'm afraid some, when they read that story or hear it explained to them, think that if they are persistent with God, then he'll get rid of whatever is bothering them. You've just got to continue praying real hard. Instead, Luke is endeavoring to teach us that we should be focused on keeping God uppermost in our lives. Requesting contentment amid emphasis on consumerism and concentrating on establishing forgiving relationships in a world where payback reciprocity is the rule requires persistent pleading to the heavenly Father that we avoid engaging in standard self-oriented thinking. It is no wonder that Jesus says that we will need the Holy Spirit. And then he says that God cannot wait to give us the Holy Spirit. Just ask him, says Jesus. And that's to constitute a big part of our praying life. It's God that we have to be focused on. If we concentrate on the reign of God, then everything else in our lives will fall into place.

As Jesus continues on his way, an increasing number of narratives feature problems relating to scribes and Pharisees. Pharisees are strong on minute rules but weak on practicing good sense in applying those rules. They also struggle with having an awareness of how to express love for God. This was what Martin Luther experienced. He was brought up well on rules and regulations, but he didn't know how to love God. And then, his awakening came. According to Luke 11:37–41, the Pharisees apparently fail to note that the rules about tithing, as specified in Deut 14, terminate with due consideration for Levites, aliens, orphans, and widows. They remember the rule, but not the context in which it was given. This ends the first woe addressed to the Pharisees, who were at dinner with Jesus in a certain Pharisee's home.

After hearing several other woes pronounced, the scribes and Pharisees have had enough of Jesus and try to catch him in his talk. Forces that are hostile to Jesus will also cause trouble for the disciples, who are warned about the hypocrisy of the Pharisees. Our tendency, when we hear the translation "hypocrisy," is to think about it in the most negative sense in which we use it. I think it is good to note that in the Greek world, to use the word hypocrite meant first of all to think in terms of a play actor. If you ask an actor today about his or her approach to a character they are portraying, they may say, "I'm not a mean person. That's just in the script." Jesus did not talk about people in a mean fashion. In the long list of apparent tirades against the

Pharisees, when Jesus calls them hypocrites, especially in Matthew, he's saying in essence that they are play actors. Matthew clarifies this by saying they are seeking the plaudits of the crowds. An awareness of the cultural context in which statements that we just glibly skim over, to mask our own hostilities or negative thinking, is so very important. These terms have a different nuance. So, the disciples are warned about the hypocrisy of the Pharisees. They need not fear the threats or attacks on their persons made by hostile figures. They have only to keep God in mind. It is God who has authority to kill and cast into Gehenna—the everlasting, burning garbage dump outside Jerusalem. This saying is meant as consolation to the followers of Jesus, as encouragement to the faint-hearted, and as a warning that disaster awaits those who obstruct God's covenant program.

At this point, we have the Parable of the Rich Fool and that's found in Luke 12:13–21. Rich fool is an accurate description. The man was a fool. Jesus spoke a parable to the people in the crowd saying, "The farm of a certain rich man bore bountifully, and he figured in himself saying, 'What am I to do? I don't have any place to store my fruits.'" That's his first mistake. They are God's fruits. God owns everything that we have. He owns the universe. He also owns our congregations by the way. So, this man says, "I know what I'm going to do. I'll tear down my silos and build bigger ones." He was speaking like a real entrepreneur. He would have been a good companion for people that work on Wall Street. "And I will gather there all my grain and my goods." Everything is my, my, my. "And I will say to my soul, 'Soul, you have many goods laid up for many years. Take your rest. Eat, drink, and enjoy yourself.'" But, then God said to him, "You fool! This night your soul will be demanded back." Here, Luke uses a word that would have been used by bankers. Your note is called in tonight. "And so, everything that you have made ready, whose is it going to be? So is anyone who treasures up for himself and is not rich toward God."

As part of his instruction to the people, Jesus emphasizes the importance of thinking outside rules and regulations. Thus, he calls the crowds hypocrites for not applying their understanding of weather forecasting to evaluating the demands of the time and the implications for their cultic center—Jerusalem. Similarly, he asks, "Why don't you think for yourselves and determine what's the right course of action?" Don't you know how to determine what's right? Do you have to look to Moses? Do you have to look to the rulers of your church to know whether this or that is right? Yet, after this very dire warning that was posted in Luke 13:1–5 about the Galileans and the blood bath that was suffered at the hands of Pilate and about the eighteen people who were killed when a tower collapsed, a leader of the synagogue indirectly indicts Jesus for healing a woman on the Sabbath. Well, the ruler doesn't realize that the ax is laid at the root of the tree. Unfortunately, these leaders of religious traditions do not heed the down stroke.

At a further point on the road, Jesus receives notice from some Pharisees that Herod is out to kill him (Luke 13:31). Jesus, therefore, should change his travel plans. Jesus echoes their word *poreuou*, which means "to go." That's the word that dominates in the Travel Document. Jesus is on the go—Luke's signature word for Jesus' trip to Jerusalem. Jesus says to the people who have given him this information about Herod: "Go and tell that fox. Pay attention." And this is the directive to Herod: "I am busy exorcising demons and performing healings today and tomorrow and on the third day, I reach my goal. Besides, it's my assignment to forge on today and tomorrow and the next day for it's not customary that a prophet perishes outside Jerusalem." What does Jesus mean when he calls Herod a fox? Exegetes have spilled a lot of ink or peppered their computers with many pecks addressing this question. The popular opinion is that Jesus refers to the fox's reputation as a crafty animal. Sly. Is that inference accurate? Now keep in mind, Luke's hermeneutical device is to present you with a narrative and then explain it. Luke frequently interprets one piece of narrative with another, either in the next or a close context. Well, here it is simple to think in terms of the next narrative. So, it's important to note that Luke follows up the reply to Herod with the pronouncement about Jerusalem's habitual treatment of the prophets: "How often would I have gathered your children, as a hen gathers her chicks under her wings, but you had no interest. Look. Your house is abandoned." In short, what is Herod? He's a predator. He uses his office like a fox that kills chickens. He becomes a metaphor for Jerusalem whose authorities hunt down prophets. As we get closer to Jerusalem, narrative segments dealing with conflict between Pharisaic and legal approaches and Jesus' teaching about tradition increase in number. Jesus persists in emphasizing that the implementation of God's interests depends on having a deeper sensitivity to human needs, just as the Torah and Israel's prophets had instructed. The result is the repeated suggestion that the traditionalists' approach is inadequate, and their hostility deepens.

At Luke 17:20, the Pharisees asked Jesus when the reign of God would come. Jesus answers by noting that determination of the kingdom's arrival cannot be made on the basis of detailed scrutiny. No one will be able to say either here it is or look there it is. Jesus then explains, "Look. The reign of God is right in your midst." Jesus, by his actions in carrying out his ministry among them, exhibits the reign of God. As a succeeding narrative about the days of Noah and Lot indicates (Luke 17:22–32), again, we see that the reign of God comes in two phases. The first surrounds the earthly activity of Jesus. The second commences, when Jesus returns as the glorified human one.

There is a follow-up story in Luke 18:18–23. It is the story of a person who seeks the sort of prestige reserved for a person of extraordinary merit. It is a story filled with economic overtones. A man comes to Jesus and adopts a patronizing tone. "Good teacher. What must I do to inherit eternal life?" A big mistake. One does not do something to get an inheritance. Leaving something in a will is left to the discretion of the testator. And it is free. The man evidently needs some remedial instruction. So, Jesus takes on the role of questioner. Since he has asked about eternal life which falls under God's jurisdiction, Jesus asks the ruler, "Why do you call me good? There's no one good but God." This again is an expression of beneficence. Leaders who have renown in a community are said to be good. The epitome of this kind of exalted merit is God. No one can compete with him for that status. God determines the rules, and the leader in the community knows them well: "I've been keen on observing all of them since the time I was quite young." He treats the items, the rules, as items on a ledger sheet. And he has checked them all off. The word "kept" indicates, as we see very frequently in the papyri, a careful attention to legal matters relating to contracts and bills. But, Jesus notes that the account sheet is missing one entry. Jesus puts it this way: "You left one thing out. Sell all you have and divide it among the poor. Oh, there's one more thing. Come and join my band." We are not told how the man's inheritance turned out. All we are told is that he was quite sad, when he received Jesus' prescription for his future well-being, for he was very rich. He had so much to ponder about his accumulation of wealth and lack of concern for the poor.

Jesus presses on to Jerusalem via Jericho. He orders two of his disciples to prepare the way for a royal entrance. It is to be in keeping with the modest way Jesus entered the world at his nativity. He was born in a stable. He now enters Jerusalem on a donkey. His entry is accompanied by joyous exclamations of praise to God as supreme benefactor. They have seen how God functioned in their behalf through Jesus, who had brought glory to God through his wonderful deeds. Again, the auditors of Luke's Gospel would be taken back to the night of Jesus' birth, when the heavenly messengers declared, "Glory to God in the highest and on earth peace." Note the word glory here. That's the kind of recognition that you are to give to a great benefactor. God is the entity worth the highest renown, especially for allotting the benefit of peace to the entire earth.

All that has taken place between the birth of Jesus and his arrival in Jerusalem is the story or logos of God's outreach to Israel. The rest of the logos that is about to unfold will highlight in bold contrast the violation of every code of obligation Israel has to respond in an appropriate manner, as the disciples of Jesus had, to God's outreaching offer of peace. For the first thing that a beneficiary is to remember is to give thanks and to act in a way that will bring renown to or increase the renown of the benefactor. Yet, there is a tantalizing ray of hope in the face of potential tragedy. If the leadership would only come to its senses without delay! Today! The city could be spared the fate that will otherwise most certainly befall it. There's still yet time. Jesus had warned the city once before about its coming desolation. This was a wake-up call. The things that pertain to its peace relate to the heeding of Jesus' instruction. But, the constant obstruction of the scribes and Pharisees requires repentance. And this, they do not do. God's judgment sets in. Those who will not see, shall not see. And so, Zachariah's earlier description of Israel being directed into the way of peace (Luke 1:79) will have to undergo some change.

With the journey to Jerusalem ended at the Mount of Olives, Jesus warns his disciples of the hazards that await them in the city. They are experiencing the quiet before the storm. Satan is about to put them through a sieve, and Jesus offers a special plea that Peter's faith not give out. The gospel story began on a cosmic scale, and it is now about to climax with a crescendo. The lynching of Jesus is about to take place. Jesus has been authorized by his heavenly Father to carry out the long-designed program for Israel's deliverance from her enemies. But in an ironical shift of allegiance, Israel's representatives engage in a plot to thwart the deliverance of their own people by accepting the offer of Judas to hand Jesus over to them. Popularly, Judas' actions are thought of as treason. In fact, "traitor" is the word that is used in Luke 6:16. But here, Luke maintains connection with Isaiah's description of the servant of the Lord who is handed over. And this is in keeping with his primary theme that Jesus carries out God's plan and purpose as laid out in Israel's Scriptures. Moreover, by using the word from Isaiah, Luke lets his auditors know that the actions taken by Judas are only part and parcel of a broadly managed plot against Jesus. Judas merely facilitates the gross injustice about to be perpetrated. In keeping with the Isaianic terminology, the Eucharistic line in 1 Corinthians 11:23 ought to read, "In the night in which he was handed over." The rendering, "The night on which he was betrayed," certainly suggests a focus on Judas, who does not come into play in Paul's narrative. The religious bureaucracy is in full swing. In Luke 20:24, the Evangelist exposes the plot of the scribes and chief priests to hand Jesus over to the jurisdiction of the Roman prefect. Judas assists them in getting Pilate to do their dirty work. Without knowing it, they are carrying out Satan's objective to eliminate a competitor, who has put his field workers in disarray. After having offered Jesus jurisdiction of all earth's realms, Satan now finds himself dislodged from heaven himself.

Luke is politically astute. He knows well how religious leaders and groups seek to influence political figures through highly charged emotional outbreaks.

Through repetition of slogans, they put pressure on officials by appealing to fear of social instability and breakdown of respect for traditions. In Acts 19, for instance, an Ephesian entrepreneur named Demetrius helped ensure profits for silver craftsmen in the name of religion. He tells a gathered crowd of producers of souvenir silver shrines commemorating the deity Artemis that Paul has been responsible for diverting crowds from purchasing their wares. Politicians are very adept at using interest in religion to carry out their activities. Paul, they say, proclaims that Artemis has no real existence, thus in effect destroying their ancestral religion. In response, the crowd of craftsmen bring religion to bear in the face of economic loss with an outcry, "Great is Artemis of the Ephesians!" In hearing this, the larger populace falls into confusion and heads into the theatre to hold a public meeting. In the course of this meeting, the racist nature of the crowd comes to fore, culminating in an outcry that goes on non-stop for about two hours. "Great is Artemis of the Ephesians!" Well, an intelligent "secretary of state" now takes charge of this public meeting, restores order, and declares that Paul and his associates are neither temple violators nor revilers of Artemis. It's worth noting that our early apostles did not denigrate polytheistic religious practice.

Like the magistrate in Ephesus, Pilate, the officer of Rome finds no legal basis for the arrest of Jesus. His opponents charge Jesus with destabilizing the country, including interfering with Caesar's government by discouraging payment of taxes and by claiming to be Christ, a king. After questioning Jesus, Pilate says to the religious authorities, "I have no case." Jesus' opponents become more vehement with their accusations. Some of them say, "He upsets the public with his teaching throughout Judea." Others add more fuel to the fire by charging that Jesus incites people all the way from Galilee to Jerusalem itself. This charge was a clever ploy to put Pilate on the defensive, for Pilate was all too familiar with Galilee's reputation as a hotbed of anti-Roman dissent. Wily politician that he was, Pilate thought of some advantage that he might gain by involving King Antipas in the case, and so Jesus goes to Herod who happened to be in Jerusalem at the same time. The chief priests and scribes do not miss a beat and are on hand for the proceedings in Herod's quarters. They make fiery accusations against Jesus. Herod and his guard amuse themselves at Jesus' expense. The outcome? Herod and Pilate that very day became intimate friends, and Jesus becomes the victim of political ping pong.

Pilate endeavors to assert his political independence and holds court with the chief priests, authorities, and the public in attendance. For the second time, he says to them: "I have no case. I can't charge him with any crime." The assembled group now demands Barabbas' release. Pilate once more addresses them hoping to change their minds so that he can release Jesus. Instead, the group cries out for crucifixion. This is the ultimate penalty for crimes committed against Roman law and order. For the last time Pilate says, "But I have no case." His weak-kneed attempt to appease them baits the crowd all the more. They overwhelm Pilate with a deafening shout, "Crucify him!" There is no evidence of love for God nor for their neighbor, who has gone up and down the land of Israel as a friend to the distressed and the needy. So, hate overcomes justice, and Pilate surrenders his judicial conscience and, as we know, ends up in the Apostles' Creed. Satan appears to have had his revenge. He has been put in charge of the kingdoms of this planet. Rome has done his bidding. The chief priests and their associates have done his bidding. But, God is the Highest One, and the crucifixion becomes the high point of God's way of demonstrating the fulfillment announced in Luke's prelude.

The cross of Jesus carries the inscription: "This is the king of the Judeans." One of the two criminals alongside Jesus expresses a variation of Diabolos' temptation: "You are the Messiah, aren't you? Well, then, rescue yourself and us." His cross-mate admonishes him: "Don't you have any fear of God, seeing that you are under the same penalty along with me? We deserve it, but he has done nothing wrong." This was tantamount to saying that Jesus was framed. There was no case at all. Then, the condemned man utters the climatic truth: "Jesus, remember me when you are inaugurated King." The name he chose was equal to Joshua, which means deliverer. Jesus answers with one of his favorite words, "today." When does the kingdom come? The reign of God is reality now. "I assure you," Jesus says, "today you will be with me in paradise." You will be with me in God's garden. The Spirit of the Lord was indeed upon Jesus. He was sending off a very bruised man with forgiveness. Extraordinary events mark God's climatic moment. Darkness comes over the land. The sun fails to shine. And wonder of wonders, the great veil in front of the holiest part of the temple is torn. In the midst of all this, Jesus musters his strongest voice. He has not forgotten his first visit to the temple, nor his very first vow. And so, with his very last breath, he cries out: "Father, into your hands I commend my spirit." Greatness, linked with beneficence, was writ large on that day.

The centurion in charge of the crucifixion proceedings recited his own verdict. He had heard the words of Jesus to the criminal, and he pondered the manner in which Jesus took his dying breath. It was a mark of unusual piety. Piety and uprightness were the marks of a renowned benefactor. The centurion blends the two ideas. "No doubt about it. This man was upright." He doesn't say he was innocent. With the word dikaios frequently used in inscriptions honoring benefactors of the state for their generous contributions to the public welfare or faithful performance in office, this Roman officer pronounces the highest accolade. When Caesar Augustus is about to close his state of the union message to the Roman people, a message that he had inscribed on stone in many places throughout the Roman Empire, he said, "I was proud especially of the honor that was bestowed on me, as one who was pious and upright." So, Luke states in effect, by using the Roman officer's words, that God deserves recognition for extraordinary performance through this crucified man. Thus, the crucifixion of Jesus is interpreted by Luke as an event managed by God's controlling hand. This is a fundamental part of the arrival of the great day of the

Lord, which we will see further expressed at Pentecost in Acts 2. God's promised salvation comes to fruition in this event. While the hour for the opposition had indeed arrived, in the end, the triumph of the opposition was destined to last only a brief time.

On the third day, Jesus appeared to two disciples on the road to Emmaus but notice what happens there is not the biggest thing. The biggest thing is what happened at the crucifixion, namely, that God was in charge of Jesus' destiny. And that destiny included being strung up, because of the opposition of God's own people. And now, on the third day, Jesus appears to two disciples. They did not recognize him but described him as a person of exceptional merit. They said he was one who functioned well not only in terms of his words but also in his deeds. After declaring that his grave was found empty, they said that Jesus was nowhere to be found. Jesus then chides them for not believing the Scriptures, which record the fate of the Messiah, who obligates himself to pay the price for total dedication to God's plan and purpose for Israel. One who fills that bill must suffer. All true prophets are treated that way. In short, Christ, the Messiah, is the hermeneutical key for understanding the Scriptures.

Jesus recites the same message to the eleven apostles and those who were in their company in Luke 24:44–47. He observes, "God declares in writing that the Messiah must suffer and then rise from the dead on the third day. Moreover, God declares that in the name of the Messiah, forgiveness of sins, accompanying repentance, is to be proclaimed to all peoples." Jesus adds, "I am sending upon you the promise of my Father." The promise embraces the arrival of the Holy Spirit. The Holy Spirit will direct their mission: "But do not go off on your own. Stay quietly in Jerusalem until you are empowered from on high with the ability to function."

In Acts 2:38, Luke reproduces the directive to proclaim repentance and forgiveness of sins. Repentance means to admit that your current way of thinking may not be aligned with God's purpose and then to adopt an entirely new way of looking at how you relate to God. Because of their fixation on traditional ways of relating to God, the Judeans had become hostile to Jesus, who focused on God's interest in reaching out to the estranged and the poor. Those were the very persons and entities that they had marginalized—outsiders, publicans and sinners, Samaritans, and people of other nationalities. They are to renounce such thinking and practice, be baptized and confess that they wish to be in

Frederick W. Danker

the company of Christ and to follow his way. The door to forgiveness will be open. This is the way to be saved or rescued from a perverse generation. It is a remarkable message. Despite the most glaring case of rejection of God's outreach to Israel, now through Jesus Christ, God announces amnesty. The Spirit of God that directed Jesus at Nazareth is in full action at this moment in Jerusalem. This is the message to the people of Israel.

In a second major speech in Acts, Peter tells an audience of Israelites that they were certainly wrong in preferring a murderer to the founder of life. But, he opens the door to a new future by telling them that they and their leaders acted in ignorance. So, he says repent from the way of thinking that led you into this and receive the wiping out of your sins. He goes on to say that they are privileged as Abraham's descendants to be the first to hear this message after Jesus' resurrection. Despite their participation in a most evil deed, they learn that they can participate in being the source of blessing to all the families on the earth. The proclamation fits Peter's words to the leaders and elders of the people: "There is no other name under heaven given people, whereby God has designed to save us" (Acts 4:12).

The long speech of Stephen recorded in Acts 7 is included to introduce Saul of Tarsus. It also describes a recurring habit of hostile thinking that has led to action against God's prophets on the part of Israelites at various periods in Israel's history. You can see how ill-conceived is the suggestion that you have any kind of anti-Judaism in Luke's Gospel or in the book of Acts. Much of the speech is devoted to reprimand subversive action taken against Moses. The description thus becomes a preface to the dramatic events that are shortly to be recorded in Luke's story of Saul—determined attacker of Jesus turned God's ambassador of the resurrected Messiah.

In Acts 9:15, Saul, also later called Paul, has his future defined for him by Jesus. He is to bear the name of Jesus before the nations, before kings, and before Israelites. In Acts 13:47, he says of himself and his associates that they have been appointed to spread God's story to the Gentiles. Paul sets forth this assignment by Jesus in words from Isaiah 49:6: "I have appointed you as a light to the Gentiles to reach out with salvation to the ends of the earth." Earlier, Simeon had focused on the prestige that Israel would enjoy, when the Gentiles received the message. Paul and his company are quite evidently in complete agreement with Simeon's announcement of God's plan. To Paul, Jesus was to be the instrument of salvation for all peoples.

The book of Acts records the successes of Jesus' heralds, as well as the many obstacles placed in front of them, as they endeavored to reach Israelites and Gentiles. Thus, the story of Jesus' fortunes during his ministry is replicated in the apostolic ministry. For Jesus had frequently said to his disciples, "You follow me, and you will encounter hazards." At Antioch of Pisidia, Paul makes a proclamation that echoes one made earlier in Jerusalem by Peter. This speech not only emphasizes the resurrection of Jesus, but also echoes Israel's privilege to have priority in hearing the good news: "My brothers, you descendants of Abraham's family, and others who fear God, to us the message of this salvation has been sent" (Acts 13:26 NRSV). Judeans would throw obstacles in front of Paul and his companions there, as well as at Thessalonica, Berea, Corinth, Ephesus, and finally in Jerusalem.

But, Luke indicates that God has the final word. In the last chapter of Acts, Paul is under house arrest with some privileges granted him. He invites some of the leading Judeans over for a discussion. After this initial gathering, all parties agree to meet again. Many more attended, and Paul spoke about Jesus' role in God's reign. Some were persuaded by what Paul presented, but others were not convinced. Before the audience adjourned,

Paul quoted a piece from Isaiah 6:9–10 that speaks about Israel hearing but lacking understanding which would lead to Jerusalem lying in ruins. The citation is made by Paul as a wake-up call to carry out Israel's assignment to the nations. In any case, says Paul, "God's saving outreach has been made known to the Gentiles. They will hear." These last words imply that even though many in Israel will not live up to their obligation to reach all the nations with the Abrahamic covenant, Paul argues that he and his associates have been faithful in carrying the assignment out. Thus, God, through them, keeps the promises he made to Abraham. The people Paul is meeting with enjoy a grand opportunity to bring great prestige to Israel. Thus, her glory is in reaching out to the nations. What Luke stated in his prologue to the Gospel has come to pass. God emerges as the fulfiller of Israel's destiny. He is the supreme politician, with Jesus second in command, and he is victor over Diabolos.

The followers of Jesus had won out over, for example, a deity, well one who started out as a physician and ended up as a deity, Asklepios. Now, Asklepios was praised as a healer in antiquity. And this is what was said of him:

> In those very days (our God Asklepios) revealed to a certain blind man named Gaius to come to the base (of the statue)

Frederick W. Danker

and worship, then to go from the right to the left and to place his five fingers on the base and to lift up his hand and hold it to his eyes; and his sight was clear as the crowd stood by and rejoiced with him, because life-giving powers showed themselves in the presence of our Augustus Antoninus.

God revealed to Lucius, afflicted with pleurisy, and given up by everyone, to come and take ashes from the altar to the Three Gods, and mix them up well with wine and to apply the mixture to the afflicted area. And he was healed and gave thanks publicly to God, and the people rejoiced with him.

To Julian, who was spitting blood and who was given up by everyone, God revealed that he should come and take from the altar to the Three Gods fine seeds and eat them with honey for three days. And he was healed and came to give thanks publicly before the people.

To Valerius Aper, a blind soldier, God revealed that he should go and take the blood from a white rooster and mix it with honey and compound a poultice and rub it in his eyes for three days. And he regained his sight and went and gave thanks publicly to (our) God.[5]

So, that's one against whom the apostles had to compete in their ministries and here is one final one. This is Isis' autobiography inscribed on stone. The following was copied from a stele in Memphis, Egypt:

I am Isis, mistress of every place, and I was instructed by Hermes, and with the help of Hermes I discovered letters,

5. Danker, *Benefactor*, 194.

both sacred and demotic[6], that everything might not be written in the same way.

I have founded laws for humanity, and I have legislated what no one has the right to alter.

I am the oldest daughter of Kronos.

I am the wife and sister of King Osiris.

I am the discoverer of the fruits (of the earth) for all humanity.

I am the mother of Horus the King.

I am the one who completes the constellation of the Dog.

I am the one whom women call their God.

For me the city of Bubastis was built.

I separated heaven from earth.

I mapped the path of the stars.

I ordained the path of the sun and moon.

I invented maritime commerce.

I made justice strong.

I brought together woman and man.

I ordained that a woman bring forth a child to the light after nine months.

I ruled that parents be loved by their children.

I set the penalty for parents who lack affection.

I, with the help of my brother Osiris, put a halt to cannibalism.

I introduced humanity to mystery rites.

I taught reverence for the images of the gods.

I founded the precincts of the gods.

I broke the reign of tyrants.

6. The term "demotic" indicates popular or ordinary language.

I put a stop to homicide.

I made it a matter of course that men be attracted by women.

I made equity stronger than gold and silver.

I ruled that truth is beautiful.

I initiated marriage contracts.

I ordained different speech for Greeks and Non-Greeks.

I made it possible for the good and the shameful to be distinguished by nature.

I made nothing more awesome than the oath one takes.

I ordained that anyone that plots unjustly against others shall be put in the power of the victim of the plot.

I ordained penalties for those who commit crimes.

I legislated mercy for suppliants.

I determined the penalty for those who avenge themselves legally. With me justice prevails.

I am mistress of the rivers, the winds, and the sea.

No one wins glory without my decision.

I am mistress of war.

I am mistress of the lightning.

I calm or enrage the sea at will.

I am in the rays of the sun.

I am in attendance at the passage of the sun.

Whatever I decree finds fulfillment.

To me all things give way.

I liberate the prisoners.

I am mistress of the sailed sea.

I make the sailable unsailable, as I see fit.

I founded enclosures of cities.

I am called "The Formulator of Rights."

I have brought islands up from the depths to the light.

I am mistress of the thunder.
I overcome that which is destined.
To me destiny gives ear.
Hail, Egypt, my Motherland.[7]

Again, this was the kind of competition that the apostles encountered throughout their mission to polytheistic Gentiles. From Rome, Paul "welcomed all who came to him, proclaiming the kingdom of God and teaching about the Lord Jesus Christ with all boldness and without hindrance" (Acts 28:30–31 NRSV). And so, you see how Luke ends his twin work with this note, that God is supreme, and God will win.

7. Danker, *Benefactor*, 198–99.

SELECTED WORKS OF
FREDERICK W. DANKER

Benefactor: Epigraphic Study of a Graeco-Roman and New Testament Semantic Field. St. Louis: Clayton Publishing House, 1982.

A Century of Greco-Roman Philology: Featuring the American Philological Association and the Society of Biblical Literature. Atlanta: Scholars Press, 1988.

The Concise Greek-English Lexicon of the New Testament (with Kathryn Krug). Chicago: University of Chicago Press, 2009.

Creeds in the Bible. Biblical Monographs Series. St. Louis: Concordia, 1966.

"The Endangered Benefactor in Luke-Acts." Pages 39–48 in *SBLSP* 20. Edited by Kent Harold Richards. Chico, CA: Scholars Press, 1981.

A Greek-English Lexicon of the New Testament and Other Early Christian Literature. 3rd ed. Chicago: University of Chicago Press, 2000.

"Imaged through Beneficence." Pages 57–67 in *Reimaging the Death of the Lukan Jesus*. Edited by Dennis D. Sylva. Athenaums Monografien. Frankfurt am Main: Anton Hain, 1990.

Invitation to the New Testament Epistles IV: A Commentary on Hebrews, James, 1 and 2 Peter, 1, 2, and 3 John, and Jude. Doubleday New Testament Commentary Series. New York: Knopf Doubleday, 1980.

Jesus and the New Age: A Commentary on St. Luke's Gospel. Minneapolis: Fortress, 1988.

"Lexical Evolution and Linguistic Hazard." Pages 1–31 in *Biblical Greek Language and Lexicography: Essays in Honor of Frederick W. Danker.* Edited by Bernard A. Taylor, John A. L. Lee, Peter R. Burton, and Richard E. Whitaker. Grand Rapids: Eerdmans, 2004.

Luke. Proclamation Commentaries. Minneapolis: Augsburg Fortress, 1985.

Multipurpose Tools for Bible Study. Rev. and expd. ed. with CD-ROM. Minneapolis: Fortress, 2003.

Second Corinthians. Augsburg Commentary on the New Testament. Minneapolis: Augsburg Fortress, 1989.

FREDERICK W. DANKER DEPOSITORIUM
Overton Memorial Library
Heritage Christian University

Frederick W. Danker (1920–2012)

In April 2010, Dr. Frederick W. Danker informed the staff of the Overton Memorial Library that he would be gifting his entire personal library and papers to the library. The process officially began in October 2010 and continued until shortly after his death in February 2012. Housed within the Danker Depositorium are files of research conducted by Professor Danker, personal correspondence, published and unpublished writings of Dr. Danker, and memorabilia from his home and office.

Dr. Frederick W. Danker's gifts to the Overton Memorial Library included several works important to the history of New Testament lexicography, such as the initial Greek-German volume by Erwin Preuschen, the first Greek-English volume by W. F. Arndt and F. W. Gingrich, and the latest edition of *The Concise Greek-English Lexicon of the New Testament* by F. W. Danker with Kathryn Krug. Krug, of Columbia, Kentucky, contributed proof pages from both the third edition of *A Greek-English Lexicon of the New Testament and Other Early Christian Literature* and *The Concise Greek-English Lexicon of the New Testament*.